*Congressional Research Service*

# House Committee Chairs: Considerations, Decisions, and Actions as One Congress Ends and a New Congress Begins

Judy Schneider
Specialist on the Congress

Michael L. Koempel
Senior Specialist in American National Government

October 25, 2012

Congressional Research Service

7-5700

www.crs.gov

RL34679

CRS Report for Congress ————————————————————

*Prepared for Members and Committees of Congress*

# Summary

A committee chair serves as the leader of a committee, with responsibility for setting the course and direction of the panel for committee members and the House and for managing a large professional and paraprofessional staff. The senior committee staff should ensure the chair's goals are carried out effectively.

Once a committee chair is selected during the post-election transition period, he or she, often in consultation with others, makes a series of decisions and takes a series of actions. Some actions complete a committee's duties in the Congress just ending, while other actions are taken in anticipation of the new Congress and then in the new Congress. Some decisions are related to the committee's policy calendar; others to the committee's administrative functions; others to the chair's responsibilities during committee sessions; others to the role of committee members; others to the relationship with the committee's ranking minority member, other chairs, and party leaders; and still others related to subcommittee leaders. Many decisions are made with a deadline imposed by House rules.

Specifically, a committee chair controls the selection of committee staff, authorizes expenditures from the committee budget, establishes operational and ethics policies, determines committee travel allocations, decides the content of the committee website, and is responsible for administration of the committee's rooms, paperwork, and other operations. Most committees entrust the drafting of the budget to the committee chair, although a committee's minority party members seek to ensure that they receive an appropriate allocation of resources. Before the chair introduces a funding resolution, the committee approves the chair's draft budget.

The House requires its committees to adopt committee rules in an open session and to publish those rules in the *Congressional Record* and in electronic form not later than 30 days after the committee chair is elected. A chair normally proposes adopting, with amendments the chair offers, the rules under which the committee operated in the previous Congress, and also proposes the number of subcommittees for the committee.

A committee chair establishes the committee agenda, calls hearings, selects witnesses and determines the order of their testimony, presides over hearings and markups, chooses any markup vehicle and pursues an amendment strategy, prepares the committee report accompanying legislation, and discusses, or might negotiate, any of these matters with the ranking minority member. The chair maintains order and decorum during committee meetings, and takes various steps to protect the committee's jurisdiction in the referral of legislation and other matters. When a measure is reported by a committee, it is the responsibility of the committee chair to consult the party leadership to determine floor scheduling for the measure.

This report covers the period from the House's early organization meetings through the spring district work period, which normally occurs in March or April. The report will be updated after the 113th Congress convenes if House rules or practices affecting chair decisions and actions discussed here change substantively.

# Contents

# Contacts

# Introduction

Each Member serves as the leader of his or her personal office. In contrast, a Member who is a committee chair serves in addition as the leader of a committee, with responsibility for setting the course and direction of the panel for other Members and the House. A chair also has responsibility for overseeing a large professional and paraprofessional staff. While day-to-day staff management is typically entrusted to a committee staff director, all senior committee staff are operational managers who should ensure that all of the duties and activities supporting a chair's goals are carried out effectively.

Once a committee chair is selected during the post-election transition period, the chair, often in consultation with others, makes a series of decisions and takes a series of actions. Some of the decisions are related to the committee's policy calendar; others to the committee's administrative functions; others to the chair's responsibilities during committee sessions; others to the role of committee members; others to the relationship with the committee's ranking minority member, other chairs, and party leaders; and still others related to subcommittee leaders.

This report addresses some of the critical matters a House committee chair confronts from the time of the early organization meetings in November to approximately the spring district work-period in March or April. The report is divided into the following sections: Transition, Administrative Matters, Committee Organization, Committee Procedure and the Role of a Chair, Procedural Tools for Committee Chairs, Floor Consideration and the Role of a Chair, and Legislative Issues and Agenda. Each section is divided into more specific topics. Actions with an identifiable deadline appear in *italics*.

This report contains numerous citations to House rules, which may be found, along with the parliamentarian's notes, in *Constitution, Jefferson's Manual, and Rules of the House of Representatives of the United States, One Hundred Twelfth Congress.*[1] An explanatory document of House rules and precedents, arranged by subject-matter, is *House Practice: A Guide to the Rules, Precedents, and Procedures of the House.*[2] The Congressional Research Service (CRS) maintains a wide-ranging set of reports—both in format or coverage and in subject matter—on the legislative process and congressional procedures, including the budget process and budget procedures. It has a similarly wide range of reports on each of hundreds of legislative issues. All CRS reports are available on the CRS website, http://crs.gov.

The Office of the Parliamentarian is the official source of parliamentary advice for committees, although parliamentarians do not attend committee meetings to assist the chair, unlike their service to the presiding officer during a meeting of the House. CRS's specialists and analysts on Congress also provide confidential parliamentary assistance and training for committee and subcommittee chairs, majority and minority members, and majority and minority staff. CRS policy specialists and analysts may assist committees, Members, and staff confidentially in

---

[1] U.S. Congress, House, *Constitution, Jefferson's Manual, and Rules of the House of Representatives of the United States, One Hundred Twelfth Congress*, H.Doc. 111-157, 111th Cong., 2nd sess., prepared by John V. Sullivan, Parliamentarian (Washington: GPO, 2011). Hereinafter *House Manual*.

[2] Wm. Holmes Brown, Charles W. Johnson, and John V. Sullivan *House Practice: A Guide to the Rules, Precedents, and Procedures of the House* (Washington: GPO, 2011). The authors are former parliamentarians of the House. See also CRS Report RL30787, *Parliamentary Reference Sources: House of Representatives*, by Richard S. Beth and Megan Suzanne Lynch.

framing policy issues, developing legislative options, planning hearings, providing written and oral policy and legislative analyses at all stages of the legislative process, and appearing as nonpartisan witnesses at hearings.

# Transition (Early Organization to Swearing-in)

The House routinely meets for so-called early organization in November, just a week or so after the election, with organizational activities continuing into December and even into January or later.[3] The November meetings typically occur simultaneously with the orientation activities planned for Members-elect, and might overlap with a so-called lame-duck session.[4]

## Selection of Chairs and Committee Members

The "steering committee" for each party (the House Democratic Caucus and the House Republican Conference), or the specific party entity responsible for committee assignments, traditionally is constituted during the early organization meetings. Party rules govern each party's process for selecting committee members and designating committee and subcommittee chairs or ranking members. If one or more committee chairmanships are contested or open,[5] the majority party's steering committee may conduct interviews during early organization meetings.[6] Each party's steering committee also makes most committee assignment recommendations during early organization, although that process may take longer as the majority and minority parties negotiate committee party ratios.[7] In some instances, the party's leader—the Speaker or minority leader—is the appointing official for members, or some members, of certain committees; the Speaker, as his or her party's leader, is the appointing official for certain chairs.[8]

The Democratic Caucus and Republican Conference meet to confirm the recommendations of their respective steering committees and party leaders. The majority party tries to complete the chairmanship selection process during this transition period. The official election of Members to committees occurs after the new Congress convenes, with the adoption of one or more House resolutions making committee assignments recommended by the party caucuses. These

---

[3] *House Manual*, § 1126, pp. 1015-1018. See CRS Report RS21339, *Congress's Early Organization Meetings*, by Judy Schneider.

[4] For an extensive examination of the occurrence, duration, and actions of lame-duck sessions, see CRS Report RL33677, *Lame Duck Sessions of Congress, 1935-2010 (74th-111th Congresses)*, by Richard S. Beth and Jessica Tollestrup.

[5] Although a chair vacancy may occur for a number of reasons, House Rule X, cl. 5(c)(2) limits Members to service of three consecutive Congresses as chair of the same committee or subcommittee. Party rules may also affect chairs' service.

[6] See CRS Report RS21165, *House Standing Committee Chairs and Ranking Minority Members: Rules Governing Selection Procedures*, by Judy Schneider.

[7] A House rule limits Members to service on two standing committees and four subcommittees of standing committees, although this rule is sometimes tacitly waived in House agreement to committee assignment resolutions. House Rule X, cl. 5(b)(2). In addition, party rules place restrictions not found in House rules on committee assignments, for example, by designating assignment to certain committees as an exclusive assignment. Delegates and the Resident Commissioner are treated as Members in the making of committee assignments. Rule III, cl. 3. See CRS Report 98-151, *House Committees: Categories and Rules for Committee Assignments*, by Judy Schneider.

[8] In addition, the Speaker appoints Members to select, joint, and conference committees "ordered by the House." House Rule I, cl. 11.

---

resolutions are voted on routinely without debate within the first few days of a new Congress. Unless a separate assignment resolution designating committee chairs is offered, designation of chairs and ranking minority members, whose names appear first on their party's roster for each committee, occurs with the adoption of the committee assignment resolutions.[9]

As committee chairs are determined during early organization meetings or thereafter, the selection process for subcommittee chairs may also begin. Applicants for subcommittee chairmanships might meet with their committee's chair, or even a prospective chair. Because of the Speaker's influence, as party leader, with committee chairs over the selection of some subcommittee chairs, applicants might also consult the party leader. In the selection process for some subcommittee chairs, including those of Appropriations Committee subcommittees, the party leader may be directly involved.[10]

The Democratic Caucus and Republican Conference also discuss their internal (party) rules during the post-election transition period, possibly amend them, and adopt them. Committee chairs monitor developments in their party's organization that impact their committee's structure and operations, and might offer their own amendments to party rules to protect their panel's interests.

During the transition period, the House Rules Committee also undertakes consideration of possible modifications to the rules of the House for the new Congress. If the House is meeting in a lame-duck session, the Rules Committee might hold hearings on potential House rules changes. Outgoing chairs, retiring Members, chair candidates, and other Members may be included as witnesses. Committee chairs are often active participants in the drafting stage of changes to House rules since any changes to committee assignments (including term limits and assignment limits), committee jurisdictions, committee procedures, numbers of subcommittees, and other rules and standing orders can have a direct effect on certain, many, or all committees.[11]

*On the day it convenes,[12] the new House agrees to a simple resolution, oftentimes numbered H.Res. 5, that adopts chamber rules for the duration of the new Congress.[13]* The resolution normally is worded to adopt the rules of the previous Congress with a series of specific amendments to them, effective with the House's agreeing to the resolution.[14]

---

[9] House Rule X, cl. 5(a)(1) (resolution on standing committee assignments); Rule X, cl. 5(c) (designation of chairs); Rule X, cl. 5(a)(2) (membership of the Budget Committee); Rule X, cl. 5(a)(3) (membership of the Ethics Committee); and Rule X, cl. 11(a) (membership of the Permanent Select Committee on Intelligence). Rule X, cl. 5(e) provides for the filling of vacancies on standing committees. Membership in a party caucus or conference is required for a Member to retain his or her committee assignments. Rule X, cl. 5(b)(1) and cl. 10(a).

[10] See CRS Report 98-610, *House Subcommittees: Assignment Process*, by Judy Schneider.

[11] The Democratic Caucus and Republican Conference traditionally send letters to their respective Members in the fall before an election to solicit suggestions for House and party rules changes. The Rules Committee has also often sent a letter to all Members soliciting suggestions for House rules changes. See also CRS Report RL32661, *House Committees: A Framework for Considering Jurisdictional Realignment*, by Michael L. Koempel, and CRS Report RL34293, *Resolving House Committee Jurisdictional Disputes: A Survey of Options*, by Walter J. Oleszek.

[12] A new Congress convenes January 3 of each odd-numbered year, although Congress may set a different convening day. U.S. Const., amend. XX, § 2. For example, the 111th Congress approved legislation signed by the President establishing the convening date of the 112th Congress as January 5, 2011. P.L. 111-289.

[13] In the 110th Congress and some recent but earlier Congresses, the rules resolution was numbered H.Res. 6.

[14] See CRS Report R42395, *A Retrospective of House Rules Changes Since the 110th Congress*, by Michael L. Koempel and Judy Schneider; and CRS Report RL33610, *A Retrospective of House Rules Changes Since the 104th Congress through the 109th Congress*, by Michael L. Koempel and Judy Schneider.

(See also the "Legislative Issues and Agenda" section related to committees' planning for legislative and oversight activities that may occur during the post-election transition.)

## End-of-a-Congress Activities

As a two-year Congress ends, House rules and practice require committees to publish certain documents and to prepare records for the National Archives. These activities are usually brought to a conclusion during the post-election transition period.

### Activities Report

Under House rules, *each committee must submit an activities report to the House by December 30.*[15] This report is the fourth and final activities report required during a two-year Congress. Such a report is to contain sections summarizing a committee's legislative and oversight activities in the preceding six-month period. There are specific requirements for what is reported on oversight activities. If Congress has adjourned sine die or it is after December 15, whichever occurs first, a chair may file the report without approval by the committee so long as the report was made available to each committee member for seven calendar days and it includes any supplemental, minority, or additional views submitted by committee members.

### Committee Calendar

Although committees are not required by House rules to publish a calendar, all committees do, except for the Appropriations, House Administration, and Ethics Committees. As a "calendar" in the congressional context, a committee calendar lists all measures referred to the committee during a Congress, the committee's actions on them, and congressional action on measures the committee reported. A calendar might also include the committee's rules, a statement of the committee's jurisdiction, rosters of the committee and its subcommittees, rosters of committee staff, and other information.

### Committee Records

Committee records are the property of the House, and must be kept separate from the personal office records of a committee chair.[16] At the end of a Congress, each committee is required to transfer its noncurrent records to the clerk of the House for transfer to the National Archives.[17] Together, these two rules also establish standards for public availability of records, under certain circumstances allowing committees to determine restrictions on availability.

## Administrative Matters

A committee chair controls the selection of committee staff, authorizes expenditures from the committee budget, establishes operational and ethics policies, determines committee travel

---

[15] House Rule XI, cl. 1(d).

[16] House Rule XI, cl. 2(e)(2).

[17] House Rule VII.

allocations, decides the content of the committee website, and is responsible for administration of the committee's rooms, paperwork, and other operations.

## Committee Budget (Expense Resolution)

One of the first orders of business for a committee in a new Congress is the drafting of a committee budget to pay the expenses the panel will incur during a two-year Congress. Most committees entrust the drafting of a budget to the committee chair, although a committee's minority party members seek to ensure that they receive an appropriate allocation of resources. Typically working from the committee's budget in the previous Congress, the chair modifies the previous budget to create a funding request reflecting the committee's anticipated resource needs. The structure and content of committees' budget requests have changed very little in recent years. A committee's budget details staff salary requirements[18] and expenses, such as reimbursements, and costs for consulting services, printing, office equipment, supplies, subscriptions, travel, and other items.

Each committee meets to approve its budget request, and Members may propose changes to the draft before a vote on approval. Following a committee's approval, *the committee chair will typically introduce a House resolution, usually in late February or early March, to provide his or her committee with funding for the two years of a Congress.* Once a resolution is introduced, the chair provides electronic and printed copies of the budget request, as well as any supporting documentation, to the House Administration Committee, to which the individual committees' resolutions are referred. The chair and ranking minority member of each committee are typically invited to testify before the House Administration Committee in support of their committee's budget request.[19]

The chair of the House Administration Committee introduces an omnibus committee funding resolution, called a "primary expense resolution" in House rules. The House Administration Committee marks it up and reports it to the House. *The House traditionally acts on the omnibus committee funding resolution in late March.*[20]

House rules also allow a primary expense resolution to contain a reserve fund for unanticipated expenses of committees. The House Administration Committee makes allocations from such a

---

[18] Personnel overhead costs, such as contributions for retirement, health insurance, and life insurance, are not specifically charged to committee budgets. U.S. Congress, House Administration Committee, *Committee Handbook*; available at http://cha.house.gov/handbooks/committee-handbook. The *Committee Handbook* contains the House Administration Committee's regulations that govern expenditures of committee funds.

[19] In the 112th Congress, as in the 111th Congress, chairs and ranking minority members were requested in addition to testify before the House Administration Committee in the second session. Section 3(c) of H.Res. 147, agreed to in the House March 17, 2011. The House in the 112th Congress also adopted a resolution after convening to reduce committee, leadership, and Member office spending. See H.Res. 22, agreed to in the House January 6, 2012.

[20] House Rule X, cl. 6 provides for primary expense resolutions. Rule X, cl. 7 provides for interim funding for the period between January 3 and March 31 in each odd-numbered year. Under this rule, for each of these three months, committees are entitled to up to 9% (or a lesser amount determined by the House Administration Committee) of the total annual amount made available to them in expense resolutions in the preceding session of Congress. See CRS Report R42778, *House Committee Funding: Process and Analysis of Disbursements*, by Matthew Eric Glassman; and CRS Report RL32794, *House Committee Funding Requests and Authorizations, 104th-112th Congresses*, by Matthew Eric Glassman.

fund, subject to the Speaker's approval.[21] House rules also allow for the possibility of one or more supplemental expense resolutions.[22]

*By the 18th of each month, each committee is directed to submit to the House Administration Committee an original and two copies of a report signed by the committee chair that contains a statement of expenses, staffing information, and other details on the committee's activities during the preceding month.*[23] House rules require funds made available to a committee to be used for the activities of the committee.[24]

## Staff and Space Allocations

Decisions on the structure and organization of a committee staff rest with the committee's chair. A determination of a committee's staffing needs, including how the committee will staff its subcommittees, is integral to the creation of a committee budget. With regard to subcommittee staffing, a House rule states: " ... the chairman of each committee shall ensure that sufficient staff is made available to each subcommittee to carry out its responsibilities under the rules of the committee.... "[25] Committee chairs have implemented this requirement in different ways. Some chairs provide autonomous staff to their committee's subcommittees, while others maintain staff at the full-committee level and detail staff to subcommittees as needed. Other systems are also used.

The same House rule states: " ... the chairman of each committee shall ensure ... that the minority party is treated fairly in the appointment of ... staff."[26] Another House rule indicates that the minority party is entitled to one-third of the up to 30 so-called statutory staff provided under the rule, or 10 staff if a committee hires 30 staff.[27] Negotiation between the committee chair and the minority, presumably the ranking minority member, could result in additional staff being available to the minority.[28]

The committee's ranking minority member is ostensibly responsible for minority staff. However, there are occasions where the committee chair exerts control, for example, in authorizing travel and approving other activities detailed in committee rules or office manuals. Minority staff's "character and qualifications" must also be "acceptable" to a majority of the committee.[29]

---

[21] House Rule X, cl. 6(a) and *Committee Handbook*.

[22] House Rule X, cl. 6(b).

[23] *Committee Handbook*.

[24] House Rule X, cl. 6(e). See also Rule X, cl. 9(b) related to a committee's use of its staff solely for committee duties.

[25] House Rule X, cl. 6(d).

[26] Ibid.

[27] House Rule X, cl. 9(a). Additional rules applicable to minority staff are contained in Rule X, cl. 9(f), (g), and (h). Additional rules applicable to committee staffing are contained in Rule X, cl. 9(c) and (e). Staffing for the Appropriations Committee is covered by Rule X, cl. 9(d). A committee may also have nonpartisan staff. Rule X, cl. 9(i). A specific rule on nonpartisan staff applies to the Ethics Committee. Rule XI, cl. 3(g).

[28] An additional control on committee staff size is exercised by the Speaker: "The Speaker sets a staff ceiling for each committee which may not be exceeded unless specifically authorized by the Speaker." In addition: "Annual rates of pay may not exceed the amount specified in the Speaker's Pay Order." *Committee Handbook,* in which additional references to the Speaker's authority over the size of committee staff and their pay appear. The Speaker's Pay Order is later published in the *United States Code.* See 2 U.S.C. 60a-2a, note.

[29] House Rule X, cl. 9(a)(2).

---

Most functions performed by committee staff, and the job titles given committee staff, are similar among committees. A staff director serves as the overall manager of a committee's staff, acts as liaison between the chair and staff, and is the chair's closest policy adviser. (On the Appropriations Committee and its subcommittees, staff directors have been called clerks.) A chief counsel generally serves as the legal counsel for the committee. This staff member often may also serve as the panel's parliamentarian. If a counsel does not have the parliamentarian role, the practice of most committees is to hire a professional staff member to serve in that capacity.

Professional policy staff, also called counsel by some committees, serve as issue experts covering the policy areas over which the committee has jurisdiction. A chief clerk and other clerks, referred to as administrative staff, serve as document managers, webmasters, calendar clerks, receptionists, and the like. The committee majority negotiates with the minority regarding the division of administrative support activities.

In addition to the monthly expense report mentioned above, *each committee chair certifies a payroll certification form for the committee and transmits it to the Human Resources Office no later than the 18th day of each month.*[30] With the approval of the House Administration Committee, a committee chair is also responsible for signing any contracts for consultants and authorizing staff detailed from government departments or agencies.[31]

Committees have majority and minority suites for staff. They also often have additional office space not connected to these suites. Even when a party continues in the majority, there is often some shifting of space allocated to specific committees. When the majority changes, the parties' committee staffs typically trade suites. The chair might decide the location of key staff members and the allocation of space to subcommittee staff or to other staff groups or teams.

Each committee is also provided parking permits for up to 80% of the committee's staff; 60% of the spaces provided are indoor and 40% are outdoor. The committee chair designates to whom parking spaces are allocated, and whether indoor spaces will be reserved or unreserved.[32]

## Travel

*Committee chairs prepare on a quarterly basis a consolidated report of spending for foreign travel by committee members and employees and provide the report to the clerk of the House.*[33] A House rule governs foreign travel and requires committee members and staff to report to a committee's chair within 60 days of completing foreign travel.[34]

## Website

Each committee has a website, and each committee's website is different. Decisions on its design, content, and the minority's input reside with a committee's chair. The minority, and individual

---

[30] *Committee Handbook.* The Human Resources Office is a part of the Office of the Chief Administrative Officer.

[31] Ibid.

[32] Ibid.

[33] *Committee Handbook.*

[34] House Rule X, cl. 8.

subcommittees, are entitled to separate pages that are linked to a committee's website and are accessible only from the committee's website.

Committees may not include political or campaign information on their website or link to any campaign or political party website. Committees are restricted in the URL they may use. Committee websites must also comply with the House Administration Committee's security regulations.[35]

# Committee Organization

## Subcommittee Structure

House rules identify the maximum number of subcommittees each committee may create. No committees, except for the Appropriations Committee and Oversight and Government Reform Committee, may have more than five subcommittees. The Appropriations Committee is allowed not more than 13 subcommittees and the Oversight and Government Reform Committee is allowed not more than seven subcommittees. Committees limited to five subcommittees are permitted to create a sixth subcommittee if it is an oversight subcommittee.[36] However, waivers enduring for a single Congress have been granted in H.Res. 5 to specific committees to allow them to have additional subcommittees.[37]

A committee chair normally proposes the number of subcommittees for the committee. However, it is the responsibility of the committee majority, acting through the committee chair and often subject to one or more party rules, to determine a committee's number of subcommittees, their size and assignment of members,[38] their jurisdiction, and their authority, that is, whether they may mark up legislation or may only conduct hearings and oversight. Further, a chair decides whether subcommittees may hire autonomous staff or obtain staff assistance from a centralized full-committee staff.

On some committees, subcommittee chairs are elected, or even selected, either by the Democratic Caucus or Republican Conference or by the respective party's leader, often in consultation with the committee chair. In addition, pursuant to chamber rules, a committee's chair and ranking minority member may serve ex officio as members of the committee's subcommittees. Some

---

[35] *Committee Handbook.* While the House Administration Committee is responsible for rules and regulations authorizing spending and other administrative matters, many services and support functions are provided by the Office of the Chief Administrative Officer (CAO), for example, information technology and office furnishings. The CAO may be contacted on the Web at http://onlinecao.house.gov, and by telephone through the First Call+, 225-8000 (fax: 226-6637).

[36] House Rule X, cl. 5(d). In the 110th Congress, the Appropriations Committee most recently reorganized to increase the number of its subcommittees to 12 from 11. See CRS Report RL31572, *Appropriations Subcommittee Structure: History of Changes from 1920 to 2011*, by Jessica Tollestrup.

[37] In the 112th Congress, the Armed Services Committee was permitted not more than seven subcommittees; the Foreign Affairs Committee, not more than seven subcommittees; and the Transportation and Infrastructure Committee, not more than six subcommittees. Section 3(k) of H.Res. 5, agreed to in the House January 5, 2011.

[38] See CRS Report 98-610, *House Subcommittees: Assignment Process*, by Judy Schneider.

---

committees' rules allow these ex officio members to be counted for a quorum or to vote, others do not.[39]

## Vice Chair

House rules direct committee chairs to designate majority-party committee and subcommittee vice chairs. No other rules seem to restrict these choices so that, for example, a vice chair need not be the most senior majority-party member of a committee or a subcommittee. While the selection of a committee vice chair rests with the committee chair, the committee chair often makes choices after consultation with party leadership. A vice chair presides over the committee or subcommittee in the absence of the chair.[40]

## Committee Rules

The House requires its *committees to adopt committee rules and to publish those rules both in electronic form and in the Congressional Record not later than 30 days after the committee chair is elected.*[41] Pursuant to both Democratic Caucus and Republican Conference rules, a committee organization meeting is usually the first meeting held by a committee, often within a very few days or weeks of the convening of a Congress. Most chairs review their committee's rules from the prior Congress and propose to adapt them to the committee's perceived needs in the current Congress. Party caucuses on each committee traditionally meet separately prior to the first official meeting of a committee.

At a committee's first meeting, committee rules are discussed, amended, and adopted. For example, quorum requirements should reflect the size and ratio of the committee, which often change from one Congress to the next. In addition, the relationship between the majority and minority parties should be made clear. How much authority should the minority or the ranking minority member have in agenda-setting and other decisions, such as the issuance of subpoenas? The use of terms such as "concurrence," "consultation," or "notification" related to agenda-setting and other decisions will describe the relationship between the majority and minority parties, or the chair and ranking minority member, and the authority of each party. Committee rules might also need to be amended to account for changes to House rules that affect committees and that were contained in H.Res. 5.

Committee rules usually manifest the role and authority of the committee chair; the ability of the majority, especially the chair, to control the agenda and legislative actions of the committee; and the desire of party leadership to move party-favored legislation through a committee and to the floor. Therefore, committees' rules tend to change only incrementally from one Congress to the next.

---

[39] House Rule X, cl. 5(b)(2)(B)(i) exempts ex officio service by a chair or ranking minority member from the limitation on subcommittee service contained in Rule X, cl. 5(b)(2)(A).

[40] House Rule XI, cl. 2(d).

[41] House Rule XI, cl. 2(a). In addition, Rule X, cl. 10(b) requires select and joint committees to comply with Rule XI, cl. 2(a). Committees also often publish their rules as committee prints.

Specific items must be addressed in committee rules, such as the selection of a regular meeting day, although committees have flexibility in drafting their rules.[42] Under House rules, the chamber's rules are the rules of its committees, and a committee's rules may not be inconsistent with chamber rules.[43] If a committee's rules are silent on a matter, House rules apply.[44]

## Administrative Matters in Support of Committee Work

Numerous functions are routine in a committee office and are undertaken by staff. Nevertheless, a committee chair can establish the environment for committee activities and direct the staff accordingly. For example, committees have assigned meeting rooms, most of which have a fixed dais. Beyond that, a chair may wish to make decisions about the standard setup for hearings, markups, and other business meetings: the location of witness and staff tables, management of live media coverage, presence of staff on the dais, the role and duties of staff at committee meetings, assistance in the maintenance of order in a room, items to be set at Members' places, and so on.

Some matters, or aspects of some matters, can be routinized through checklists, form letters, and ongoing contacts. For example, committee staff can create templates to be used in most situations for requesting the attendance of attorneys from the Office of Legislative Counsel, obtaining recording and transcription services from the Office of Official Reporters, notifications to the Capitol Police, and invitations to witnesses.

# Committee Procedure and the Role of a Chair

A committee chair establishes the committee agenda, divides work between the subcommittees and the full committee, determines procedural strategy, calls hearings, selects witnesses and determines the order of their testimony, presides over hearings and markups, chooses the markup vehicle and pursues an amendment strategy, prepares the committee report accompanying legislation, and discusses, or might negotiate, any of these matters with the ranking minority member.

## Hearings

Under House rules, *a committee chair must publicly announce the date, place, and subject matter of a hearing at least one week in advance of the date and publish the announcement in the Daily Digest section of the Congressional Record and make it publicly available in electronic form.*[45] Many hearing-related and administrative tasks need to be performed in preparation for a hearing,

---

[42] House Rule XI, cl. 2(a)(1)(C) requires committees to incorporate in their rules the "succeeding provisions" of Rule XI, cl. 2 "to the extent applicable." Rule XI is titled "Procedures of Committees and Unfinished Business."

[43] House Rule XI, cl. 1(a)(1)(A), and Rule XI, cl. 2(a)(1)(B), respectively.

[44] For example, House Rule XI, cl. 2(g) (open meetings and hearings) and Rule XI, cl. 4 (audio and visual coverage of committee proceedings) are long, detailed statements of policy and procedure. In their rules, a number of House committees summarize and reference, or simply reference, these House rules.

[45] House Rule XI, cl. 2(g)(3). This subparagraph also allows a chair to give less notice with the "concurrence of the ranking minority member" or by "majority vote" of the committee.

---

many of which are undertaken by committee staff.[46] The committee chair is responsible for the selection and invitation of witnesses to testify, including determining the order in which they will testify and whether they will appear alone or as part of a panel. The minority, however, is entitled under the rules to also call witnesses.[47] A committee chair may decide whether or not to swear a witness.[48] A chair might also decide who for the majority should lead questioning of a particular witness or on a particular subject, or what alternatives to member-by-member questioning to pursue.[49] House rules require a committee chair to maintain order and decorum during committee proceedings—recognizing committee members, responding to breaches of decorum by a witness or of professional ethics by a witness's counsel, and maintaining order in the audience.[50]

Chairs should make an opening statement to reiterate the purpose of a hearing[51] and to set a tone for the hearing, and then speak last to thank witnesses for their testimony.[52] Chairs also often send thank-you letters to witnesses after their appearance.[53]

## Markups and Reporting

Committee chairs have primary authority for the scheduling of a markup,[54] selection of a markup vehicle,[55] and conduct of a markup. Many committee chairs caucus with their party's committee

---

[46] See CRS Report 98-488, *House Committee Hearings: Preparation*, by Christopher M. Davis.

[47] House Rule XI, cl. 2(j)(1). See CRS Report RS22637, *House Committee Hearings: The "Minority Witness Rule"*, by Christopher M. Davis.

[48] It is unlawful for a witness to make a false statement whether sworn or not (18 U.S.C. 1001).

[49] For example, House Rule XI, cl. 2(j)(2)(B) and (C) authorizes committees to adopt in their rules alternative means of questioning witnesses than the five-minute rule.

[50] House Rule XI, cl. 2(k)(4).

[51] House Rule XI, cl. 2(k)(1).

[52] Committees must also publish in electronic form the so-called truth-in-testimony disclosures made by witnesses. House Rule XI, cl. 2(g)(5).

[53] House Rule XI, cl. 1(c) provides authority for committees to print hearings. Rule XI, cl. 2(e)(4) directs committees to make their publications available in electronic form to the "maximum extent feasible," and cl. 2(e)(5) directs committees to the "maximum extent practicable" to provide audio and video coverage of every hearing and meeting and to maintain recordings, both in a manner consistent with public access. Rule XIII, cl. 4(c) contains a so-called layover rule related to the availability of printed Appropriations Committee hearings. In addition to the *Committee Handbook*, the Committee on House Administration website contains a section of guidance labeled "Transparency Initiatives," available at http://cha.house.gov/legislation/schedule/transparency-initiatives.

See also U.S. Congress, Committee on House Administration, news release, "LOC Launches New Site to Webcast House Committee Proceedings," Feb. 2, 2012, available at http://cha.house.gov/press-release/loc-launches-new-site-webcast-house-committee-proceedings; and news release, "Clerk Launches New Site for House Documents," January 17, 2012, available at http://cha.house.gov/press-release/clerk-launches-new-site-house-documents.

[54] House Rule XI, cl. 2(g)(3) disallows a committee meeting to be held prior to the "third day on which members have notice." This subparagraph also allows a chair to give less notice with the "concurrence of the ranking minority member" or by "majority vote" of the committee.

[55] House Rule XI, cl. 2(g)(4) requires the text of the markup vehicle to be available at least 24 hours in advance of a markup meeting; a shorter availability is possible under this subparagraph if the chair has received approval for a shorter notice under clause 2(g)(3), as the previous note explains. The section-by-section analysis of H.Res. 5 (112th Cong.) indicated: "This provision is intended to ensure that members have the text of the measure or matter in sufficient time to review the measure and draft any amendments. Accordingly, if the committee is considering a committee print, or the Chair of a committee intends to use an amendment in the nature of a substitute as the base text for purposes of further amendment, circulation of that text will satisfy this requirement." Rep. David Dreier, "Rules of the House," insert, *Congressional Record*, vol. 157, January 5, 2012, p. H13.

---

members prior to a markup to discuss strategy at the markup. As with hearings, many tasks need to be performed in preparation for markups, although many of them are conducted by staff.[56]

During markup, a committee chair often serves as the primary spokesman (or designates the primary spokesman) for or against amendments offered to the markup vehicle. A committee chair also decides whether to vote first or last on a recorded vote. (Chairs usually make a one-time decision, which they adhere to on most or all votes in all of their committee's markups.) At the end of a markup, when a committee votes to report a measure, it is incumbent upon the chair, pursuant to House rules, to report the measure "promptly" and to take the "steps necessary" to secure chamber consideration of the measure.[57]

The committee chair is responsible for preparation of the committee report to accompany legislation reported from the committee as well as other committee reports and documents on other committee activities.[58] A committee must in addition post in electronic form within 48 hours votes taken in markup and the text of amendments adopted.[59]

Outgoing chairs usually recommend to their successors that they hire or charge a specific staff member with primary responsibility for procedural matters, since a chair must follow and enforce parliamentary procedures during sittings of the committee, sometimes with little or no notice of the parliamentary issue raised. In addition, a chair may need advice on parliamentary rulings and strategy before, during, and after a committee meeting. Attorneys from the Office of the Parliamentarian of the House do not attend committee meetings, although they meet with or take calls from committee members and staff related to committee meetings. Confidential parliamentary assistance and training for committee and subcommittee chairs, majority and minority members, and majority and minority staff is also available from CRS.

Outgoing chairs also recommend to their successors that they have a procedural script so that a chair has ready access to language to initiate or respond to common parliamentary matters, such as recognition of a committee member to offer an amendment, the reservation of a point of order, or a request for a recorded vote. The chair and committee staff also attempt to anticipate possible procedural roadblocks prior to a markup and to prepare responses that will allow the chair and the majority party to prevail in their legislative objectives.[60]

---

[56] For overviews of the markup process, see CRS Report 98-168, *House Committee Markup: Preparation*, by Judy Schneider; and CRS Report RL30244, *The Committee Markup Process in the House of Representatives*, by Judy Schneider. For an extensive manual on the markup process, which includes sample scripts, see CRS Report R41083, *House Committee Markups: Manual of Procedures and Procedural Strategies*, by Michael L. Koempel and Judy Schneider.

[57] House Rule XIII, cl. 2(b).

[58] House rules pertaining to committee reports are found generally in House Rule XIII, clauses 2 - 6. The House rule on the right of a Member to file supplemental, minority, or additional views appears at Rule XI, cl. 2(l). Additional House rules pertaining to reports of the Ethics Committee are found Rule XI, cl. 3. See also CRS Report 98-169, *House Committee Reports: Required Contents*, by Judy Schneider.

[59] House Rule XI, cl. 2(e)(1)(B) and cl. 2(e)(6), respectively.

[60] See CRS Report RS20308, *House Committee Markups: Commonly Used Motions and Requests*, by Judy Schneider; and CRS Report R41083, *House Committee Markups: Manual of Procedures and Procedural Strategies*, by Michael L. Koempel and Judy Schneider.

## Subcommittee Authority

A committee chair usually works with other majority-party members of the committee, and on occasion with minority-party members, to decide what role subcommittees will play in the committee's work. Some questions about this role are: Will subcommittees be authorized to mark up legislation or solely hold hearings? Will the subject matter of legislation influence that decision? Will the role of subcommittees be uniform for all of a committee's subcommittees? If subcommittees mark up legislation, what form will be used to report their work to the full committee—a letter to the full committee detailing subcommittee action, a formal subcommittee report, the introduction of legislation reflecting the subcommittee's action, or some other method? Will subcommittees be named in committee rules? What role(s) and authority of subcommittees will be detailed in committee rules, or will the rules be silent on these matters?

As suggested earlier in this report, different committees have differing relationships with their subcommittees, and, even within one committee, different subcommittees might have differing roles.[61]

# Procedural Tools for Committee Chairs

Rules and practices of the House vest discretion with a committee chair, but he or she must be vigilant and well served by committee staff in using this discretion.

## Maintaining Order and Decorum

As already indicated, committee chairs are responsible for maintaining order and decorum in committee proceedings. They also have parliamentary tools at their disposal to allow them to minimize delaying tactics.[62] In exercising the authority and prerogatives available, a chair seeks to strike a balance between the responsibility of the majority to govern and the rights of the minority to be heard. Some key procedures are listed here concerning questions of order that might arise in a committee session and the authority of the chair to respond to them.

- The chair has discretion to recognize Members to pose a parliamentary inquiry. He or she also has authority to decline to entertain an inquiry if, in the chair's judgment, the inquiry is not relevant to the pending question.

- The chair does not need to respond to hypothetical questions raised under the guise of a parliamentary inquiry. In addition, the chair does not need to respond to an issue until the issue is raised.

- A parliamentary inquiry may not be used to ask a question about the substance of a measure or amendment. The purpose of a parliamentary inquiry is to ask a parliamentary question.

---

[61] House Rule XI, cl. 1(a)(1)(B) states: "Each subcommittee is a part of its committee and is subject to the authority and direction of that committee and to its rules, so far as applicable."

[62] House rules explicitly provide two privileged motions in committee, related to recessing the committee and dispensing with the first reading of a measure. House Rule XI, cl. 1(a)(2).

- The chair rules on points of order. Debate on a point of order is at the discretion of the chair. A ruling on a point of order, however, may be appealed and the appeal may be tabled.[63]

## Protecting Committee Jurisdiction

In the early days of a new Congress, when dozens of bills are introduced each day that the House is in session, committees must pay special attention to referral decisions to ensure that referrals do not adversely affect their jurisdiction over specific measures or over subject matter generally. By March 31, 2011, 1,306 bills, 53 joint resolutions, 32 concurrent resolutions, and 196 simple resolutions had been introduced in the House. Pursuant to House rules on referral of legislation, these measures were referred to one or more House committees, with a primary committee designated for measures referred to more than one committee.[64] In addition to the normal complexities involved in determining committees' jurisdiction over a measure, the creation of a permanent Homeland Security Committee, which has some overlapping jurisdiction with other standing committees, has added uncertainties to referral decisions.[65]

Concerns or disputes, and suggested solutions, such as re-referral or sequential referral, need to be acted on quickly, potentially with negotiations between committees and by being brought to the Speaker's attention since referrals are made on the Speaker's authority under House rules.[66]

# Floor Consideration and the Role of a Chair

When a measure is reported by a committee, it is the responsibility of the committee chair to consult the party leadership to determine floor scheduling for the measure.[67] There are two

---

[63] Two points of order that tend to arise in legislative committees' markups relate to House Rule XVI, cl. 7 (germaneness) and Rule X, cl. 1 (committee jurisdiction).

[64] House Rule X, cl. 1 contains the principal statement of committees' legislative jurisdiction. These jurisdictional statements are supplemented by precedents, memoranda of understanding, Speaker's announcements, and other jurisdictional explanations. Rule XII, cl. 2 is the principal House rule guiding the Speaker in the referral of bills and resolutions, including to special committees appointed by the Speaker with the approval of the House. Additional referral authority for the Speaker is contained in Rule XIV, cl. 2. Guidance to the Speaker on the referral of specific types of measures or matters, such as private bills, is contained in Rule XII, cl. 3, cl. 4, and cl. 6.

The jurisdiction of the Permanent Select Committee on Intelligence appears at Rule X, cl. 11(b). The Rule X, cl. 1 jurisdiction of the Ethics Committee is supplemented by Rule XI, cl. 3(a). Additional explanation of the House Administration Committee's jurisdiction over House officers appears in Rule II.

Additional jurisdictional protections exist in House rules for two committees. The Ways and Means Committee's jurisdiction is protected by Rule XXI, cl. 5. The Appropriations Committee's jurisdiction is protected by Rule XXI, cl. 4. The authorization-appropriation division of labor is protected in Rule XXI, cl. 2.

[65] The House has sought to deal with some of these uncertainties with memoranda of understanding, statements in the *Congressional Record*, letters inserted in the *Congressional Record*, and other mechanisms.

[66] House Rule XII, cl. 2. See CRS Report 98-175, *House Committee Jurisdiction and Referral: Rules and Practice*, by Judy Schneider. Committees also need to monitor the potential filing of a discharge petition on any measures referred to them or on special rules referred to the Rules Committee but making in order consideration of a bill referred to one or more legislative committees. House rules pertaining to the discharge process appear at Rule XV, cl. 2, and Rule XIII, cl. 1(b). See CRS Report 97-552, *The Discharge Rule in the House: Principal Features and Uses*, by Richard S. Beth.

[67] See CRS Report 98-996, *Legislative Procedures and the Legislative Agenda in the House of Representatives*, by Christopher M. Davis (out of print; available from the author); and CRS Report 95-563, *The Legislative Process on the House Floor: An Introduction*, by Christopher M. Davis.

---

principal routes to the floor: suspension of the rules, and a special rule from the House Rules Committee.

If a measure is reported or ordered reported and is fairly noncontroversial, it might qualify to be considered under suspension of the rules procedure. A committee chair might mention at markup his or her intention to seek floor consideration by that means. If the measure is deemed appropriate for suspension consideration, the chair notifies the Speaker of the House and majority leader of the his or her desire for the measure to be considered in that manner since it is within the Speaker's discretion to choose legislation to be considered under the suspension procedure.[68]

If the measure is more contentious, or does not appear appropriate for suspension consideration, a special rule can be sought. The committee chair writes a letter to the Rules Committee, often co-signed by the ranking minority member, asking the panel for a hearing on the measure. If, after consultation with the majority leadership, the Rules Committee holds such a hearing, the committee chair is traditionally the first witness to testify on behalf of the legislation, perhaps with the ranking minority member. The chair recommends the type of special rule sought for the measure's consideration, and how the special rule should address matters, such as points of order, that the chair would like the special rule to cover.

In making the motion to suspend the rules and pass a measure, or, following adoption of a special rule in the House, the chair may take, delegate, or delegate in part the role of majority floor manager. In this role, the chair determines which majority-party Members speak on a measure, and in what order, and which Members will speak in support of or in opposition to amendments that are allowed and offered on the floor.[69] The committee chair is usually responsible for choosing, for his or her party, which amendments will receive voice votes and which will require recorded votes. The chair also takes a lead in raising or debating parliamentary questions and points of order.

Finally, if a House- and Senate-passed measure is to be reconciled by conference with the Senate, a committee chair works with the party leadership in selecting conferees from his or her committee and in determining the overall number of conferees to, perhaps, accommodate other committees and individual Members. The committee chair serves as the chair of the House delegation or may chair the conference.[70]

# Legislative Issues and Agenda

The time before a new Congress convenes and the time immediately afterwards are critical periods for the development of a committee's agenda—for the next months, the first session, and even for the two-year Congress. While some legislation can move quickly through committee, and perhaps through the two houses of Congress, other legislation can take many months and perhaps still not have cleared Congress before it adjourns sine die after two years.[71]

---

[68] House Rule XV, cl. 1. Two other types of legislation that are likely to be noncontroversial and handled on the floor in a expeditious manner are privileged on certain days: Rule XV, cl. 4 (District of Columbia legislation), and Rule XV, cl. 5 (private legislation).

[69] House Rule XVII, cl. 3.

[70] See CRS Report 96-708, *Conference Committee and Related Procedures: An Introduction*, by Elizabeth Rybicki.

[71] The Appropriations Committee, however, works on an annual cycle to produce 12 regular appropriations bills, or (continued...)

A committee might look back to the previous Congress, or previous Congresses, to see what groundwork has been laid through hearings and other activities, such as Government Accountability Office (GAO) evaluations requested, on subject matter within the committee's jurisdiction. A committee might also look ahead to the current or following Congress when a major, multi-year program authorization is expiring or when the committee wishes to report legislation to reform a major federal program. Action in the current Congress can save time and build momentum in the next Congress. Some committees hold retreats, sometimes with outside speakers, to help them develop their legislative agenda.

## State of the Union

The major initiatives of the President and his administration are sometimes first announced in *the annual State of the Union address, which often occurs during the third or fourth week of January.*[72] These initiatives can be new for the President, a reiteration of actions he sought in the past from Congress, an endorsement of legislative proposals originated by Members of Congress, a refocus to an existing set of programs, or an expansion or contraction of a set of programs that the President's annual budget might subsequently reflect. Many other forms of presidential initiatives are also possible, such as the issuance of executive orders.

A House committee's jurisdiction might encompass one or more presidential initiatives, and the chair and members of the committee must listen to the President's initiatives both as committee members and as individual Members representing their district and party. The chair and the committee's majority-party members are under no specific obligation to take any action on a suggestion or request of the President or on legislation subsequently transmitted by the President or his administration to Congress,[73] unless directed by the House or their party to take an action.

Considerations of whether or not to take an action, and what that action might be, could include—

- whether or not the President and Congress are controlled by the same party, or whether just one chamber is of the same party as the President,

- the President's and his administration's commitment to an initiative,

- the chair's and the committee's majority-party members' interests, priorities, and desires,

---

(...continued)

other appropriations bills covering these 12 bills, as well as supplemental and continuing appropriations bills. See CRS Report R42388, *The Congressional Appropriations Process: An Introduction*, by Jessica Tollestrup; CRS Report RL32473, *Omnibus Appropriations Acts: Overview of Recent Practices*, by Jessica Tollestrup; and CRS Report R42647, *Continuing Resolutions: Overview of Components and Recent Practices*, by Jessica Tollestrup.

[72] One practice of the House and Senate is to convene for several days on January 3, or immediately thereafter, of an odd-numbered year to swear in Members and deal with other organizational business, and then to adjourn until the week of the President's State of the Union message or, when there will be a presidential inauguration, until the week in which January 20 falls. In a presidential inauguration year, an outgoing President might submit a written State of the Union message, or he may make a broadcast farewell address to the nation. A new President might address Congress on his legislative program later in the winter. See also CRS Report R40132, *The President's State of the Union Address: Tradition, Function, and Policy Implications*, by Colleen J. Shogan and Thomas H. Neale. Another practice is to convene, organize, and then pass several pieces of legislation of high priority to the majority party.

[73] As a courtesy, a chair, ranking minority member of the President's party, a chair and ranking minority member together, or an individual Member might introduce Administration-proposed legislation "by request."

---

- House leadership and majority-party sentiments,

- minority-party views,

- a decision on which chamber of Congress should act first,

- the role of Congress and necessity for congressional action, such as the expiration of the authorization of a major federal program,

- alternatives to congressional action and potential consequences of inaction,

- other matters competing for a place on the committee's agenda,

- national, regional, local, ideological, and other political perspectives,

- public opinion,

- actions anticipated in another committee with related jurisdiction, and

- actions anticipated in the other chamber.

## President's Budget

By law, *the President transmits a budget for the U.S. government after the first Monday in January but no later than the first Monday in February.*[74] In its content, the budget will contain budget requests, proposed legislative language related to specific requests, and legislative initiatives that have budget consequences. While the President's budget is referred to the Appropriations Committee, less than 40% of new budget authority is within the jurisdiction of the committee, and it has no jurisdiction over revenues or debt. Particular budget requests and legislative initiatives, including changes to entitlement and revenue laws, are within the jurisdiction of specific legislative committees. Legislative proposals in support of the President's budget recommendations might not be submitted until much later, yet implementation of some, many, or the major initiatives in the President's budget might depend on congressional passage of legislation separate from annual appropriations bills.[75]

---

[74] When a new President is to take office, the outgoing President might submit only a brief budget document, allowing the new President to submit his own proposals for spending and revenue for the next fiscal year. See CRS Report RS20752, *Submission of the President's Budget in Transition Years*, by Michelle D. Christensen.

A broader treatment of issues of concern to Congress and its agenda during and immediately following presidential transitions can be found in CRS Report RL34722, *Presidential Transitions: Issues Involving Outgoing and Incoming Administrations*, by L. Elaine Halchin.

[75] "Appropriation—(1) Legislative language that permits a federal agency to incur obligations and make payments from the Treasury for specified purposes, usually during a specified period of time. (2) The specific amount of money made available by such language.... The House of Representatives claims the exclusive right to originate appropriation bills—a claim the Senate denies in theory but accepts in practice."

"Budget Authority—The amount of money that may be spent or obligated by a government agency or for a government program or activity. Technically, budget authority is statutory authority to enter into obligations that normally result in outlays. The main forms of budget authority are appropriations, borrowing authority, and contract authority. It also includes authority to obligate and expend the proceeds of offsetting receipts and collections. Congress may make budget authority available for only one year, several years, or an indefinite period, and it may specify definite or indefinite amounts."

From *Congressional Quarterly's American Congressional Dictionary* (Washington, DC: CQ Press, 2001), pp. 12-13 and 24-25; available online to Congress, at http://www.crs.gov/pages/glossary_a.aspx.

Many of the same considerations a committee might review related to presidential initiatives in the State of the Union address apply to the committee's activities related to matters within the committee's jurisdiction in the President's budget. In addition, a committee might want to hold hearings or undertake other actions to influence the appropriations process if it strongly supports or disagrees with specific budget requests. Some committees hold budget-themed hearings immediately or shortly after the President transmits the budget in order to hear from relevant Cabinet secretaries and agency heads and perhaps others.

## Budget Resolutions, Views and Estimates, and Appropriations

Transmittal of the President's budget has a noticeable, immediate impact on House committees. Transmittal of the budget begins a season of work taking place simultaneously in the Budget, Appropriations, and legislative, or authorizing, committees, with parallel activities occurring in Senate committees. Under the Congressional Budget Act, *Congress is expected to complete bicameral agreement on a concurrent resolution on the budget by April 15*, although it does not usually do so. Also under the Budget Act, *the House Appropriations Committee is expected to report all the annual appropriations bills by June 10*, although it does not usually do so.[76]

To prepare a concurrent resolution on the budget, the House Budget Committee holds hearings, which include appearances by the President's economic team of Cabinet and Cabinet-rank officials, and receives analyses from the Congressional Budget Office (CBO),[77] among other inputs. A critical part of the committee's information gathering is its receipt of "views and estimates reports" from each of the other House committees. Under the Congressional Budget Act and House rules, *House committees report their views and estimates to the Budget Committee no later than six weeks after the President transmits his budget, which would be no later than March 15 if the President transmits the budget on February 1.*[78]

A House committee might hold a meeting at which it considers its proposed views and estimates report, or might consider the proposed report in the course of a meeting having several agenda items. Committee chairs usually take the lead in deciding the approach to drafting the report and the drafting itself. Not all committees necessarily hold a meeting on their proposed views and estimates reports.[79] A committee's views and estimates report might take the form of a letter to the Budget Committee's chair and ranking minority member, the form of a detailed report, or another form. Sometimes majority and minority members of a committee submit separate views and estimates, and sometimes individual members of a committee submit additional or other views to supplement their committee's report.

---

[76] For a substantive overview of the congressional budget process and its relationship to the executive budget process, see CRS Report 98-721, *Introduction to the Federal Budget Process*, coordinated by Bill Heniff Jr. See also CRS Report RL30297, *Congressional Budget Resolutions: Historical Information*, by Bill Heniff Jr. and Justin Murray.

[77] Regarding the importance of CBO's baseline budget projections for the Budget Committee and other House committees, see CRS Report 98-560, *Baselines and Scorekeeping in the Federal Budget Process*, by Bill Heniff Jr.

[78] House Rule X, cl. 4(f)(1). A CBO report integral to both the Budget Committees in their preparation of a budget resolution and to legislative committees in their preparation of their views and estimates is *The Budget and Economic Outlook*. See, for example, *The Budget and Economic Outlook: Fiscal Years 2010 to 2020*, available at http://cbo.gov/ftpdocs/108xx/doc10871/BudgetOutlook2010_Jan.cfm.

[79] House Rule X, cl. 4(f)(2) directs the Ways and Means Committee to include specific recommendations on the appropriate level of public debt in its views and estimates report. The recommendations, however, are to be "made after holding public hearings."

---

A report typically includes comments on the President's budget proposals, and estimates of the budgetary impact of any legislation likely to be considered by a committee during the current session of Congress. A report might contain specific comments on direct spending within a committee's jurisdiction and could also discuss the committee's authorizations that require funding in annual appropriations measures. A views and estimates report might also comment on structural and procedural aspects of the budget that affect a committee's jurisdiction. The Ways and Means Committee's views and estimates report discusses revenues and revenue and debt legislation.

Because of the amount of work it takes for the House Appropriations Committee to consider and draft the House's annual appropriations bills, the appropriations subcommittees usually begin their hearings quickly once the President transmits the budget. Over the course of several months, each subcommittee will likely hear from relevant Cabinet officials and other agency heads; numerous executive officials who can speak to specific programs and activities; Members of Congress; and public witnesses, that is, not federal government officials or employees.

The concurrent resolution on the budget establishes total spending levels, among other provisions. The joint explanatory statement accompanying the conference report on the budget resolution contains the allocation of spending among each chamber's committees, including the House Appropriations Committee. The Appropriations Committee subdivides its allocation among its subcommittees.[80] If a budget resolution has not been finally agreed to by the House and Senate, the House might adopt a "deeming resolution," minimally making a spending allocation to the Appropriations Committee.[81] *In the absence of a budget resolution, the Appropriations Committee may begin reporting annual appropriations bills after May 15.*[82]

A budget resolution agreed to by both chambers might also contain reconciliation instructions, which are provisions directing specified committees to report legislation within their jurisdiction that changes revenues or spending, or both, by certain amounts, usually by a specified deadline. If the budget resolution agreed to by the House and Senate contains reconciliation instructions, the instructions are an order of the parent chamber to named committees to comply. In such a case, the named committees must put reconciliation on their agendas.[83]

## Expiring Authorizations

In establishing federal programs and agencies, Congress often provides an authorization for a fixed period of time.[84] A program, for example, might have a one-year authorization, requiring

---

[80] See CRS Report 98-512, *Formulation and Content of the Budget Resolution*, by Bill Heniff Jr.; and CRS Report RS20144, *Allocations and Subdivisions in the Congressional Budget Process*, by Bill Heniff Jr.

[81] See CRS Report RL31443, *The "Deeming Resolution": A Budget Enforcement Tool*, by Megan Suzanne Lynch.

[82] See CRS Report R42388, *The Congressional Appropriations Process: An Introduction*, by Jessica Tollestrup.

[83] See CRS Report 98-814, *Budget Reconciliation Legislation: Development and Consideration*, by Bill Heniff Jr.,; and CRS Report R41151, *Budget Reconciliation Process: Timing of Committee Responses to Reconciliation Directives*, by Megan Suzanne Lynch. For an explanation of changes to the budget process made in the House rules package for the 112th Congress, see CRS Report R41926, *House Rules Changes Affecting the Congressional Budget Process Made at the Beginning of the 112th Congress*, by Bill Heniff Jr.

[84] "Authorization—(1) A statutory provision that establishes or continues a federal agency, activity, or program for a fixed or indefinite period of time. It also may establish policies and restrictions and deal with organizational and administrative matters. (2) A statutory provision, as described in (1), may also, explicitly or implicitly, authorize congressional action to provide appropriations for an agency, activity, or program. The appropriations may be (continued...)

---

passage of legislation each year to continue the program, or it might have a multi-year authorization of two, three, or more years, requiring the passage of legislation only before the end of the specific number of years to continue the program.[85] Congress also sometimes passes legislation temporarily continuing a program for six months, a year, or some other period in order to give itself additional time to complete passage of new multi-year authorization legislation. These fixed-year and short-term authorizations can apply to spending programs, tax provisions, grants of legal authority, or other matters.[86]

Legislation to "reauthorize" existing programs and agencies, and legislation authorizing new programs and agencies, might also have failed to clear the previous two-year Congress, and remain as potential agenda items in the current Congress.

Ushering through Congress legislation to reauthorize programs and agencies is some of the most consequential work that legislative committees undertake each Congress. Committees may consider authorization legislation because existing authority is about to expire, new authority is needed to deal with new or newly identified issues, or for other reasons. New authorizations and major reauthorizations can consume a large amount of committees' time and effort during one or more sessions of Congress. Reauthorizations that are arguably noncontroversial, such as for some small business programs, are nonetheless important legislative products that committees must support with their time and effort to see them enacted into law.

Many provisions of the revenue code and the major entitlement programs continue in effect indefinitely. To make changes in these kinds of laws, Congress must enact new law.[87] However, some provisions of these kinds of laws are temporary, and Congress needs to enact new law to continue temporary provisions in effect.[88]

---

(...continued)

authorized for one year, several years, or an indefinite period of time, and the authorization may be for a specific amount of money or an indefinite amount ('such sums as may be necessary'). Authorizations of specific amounts are construed as ceilings on the amounts that subsequently may be appropriated in an appropriation bill, but not as minimums; either house may appropriate lesser amounts or nothing at all."

From *Congressional Quarterly's American Congressional Dictionary* (Washington, DC: CQ Press, 2001), p. 15; available online to Congress, at http://www.crs.gov/pages/glossary_a.aspx.

[85] CBO is required each January to issue reports on expiring authorizations and unauthorized appropriations. See, for example, CBO Report, *Unauthorized Appropriations and Expiring Authorizations* (Washington, DC: CBO, January 31, 2012), available at http://cbo.gov/publication/42858.

[86] Through the appropriations process, Congress may also continue programs and agencies that rely on appropriations. "The separation between the two steps of the authorization-appropriations process is enforced through points of order provided by rules of the House and Senate. First, the rules prohibit appropriations for unauthorized agencies and programs; an appropriation in excess of an authorized amount is considered an unauthorized appropriation. Second, the rules prohibit the inclusion of legislative language in appropriations measures. Third, the House, but not the Senate, prohibits appropriations in authorizing legislation. While the rules encourage the integrity of the process, a point of order must be raised to enforce the rules. Also, the rules may be waived by suspension of the rules, by unanimous consent, or, in the House, by a 'special rule.' If unauthorized appropriations are enacted into law through circumvention of House and Senate rules, in most cases the agency may spend the entire amount."

From CRS Report RS20371, *Overview of the Authorization-Appropriations Process*, by Bill Heniff Jr.

[87] For an explanation of "cut-as-you-go" affecting mandatory spending and other budget process changes in the 112th Congress, see CRS Report R41926, *House Rules Changes Affecting the Congressional Budget Process Made at the Beginning of the 112th Congress*, by Bill Heniff Jr.

[88] "Revenue—Funds collected from the public primarily as a result of the federal government's exercise of its sovereign powers. These include individual and corporate income taxes, excise taxes, duties, and mandatory social insurance receipts (such as Social Security and Medicare premiums)."

(continued...)

---

Each committee tries to anticipate and plan its work related to expiring authorizations. Among the possible consequences that a committee might consider for inaction, in addition to the possible lapse of the program or agency, are the decline of congressional control over policy; ceding of policy influence, where appropriations are necessary, to the Appropriations Committee from a legislative committee; loss of jurisdiction by a committee; and loss of influence by and support for a committee within the House.

## Committee Legislative Priorities

While the President and the executive departments and agencies are often sources of important or high-profile legislation, committee chairs and committee members, especially majority-party members, establish a committee's legislative priorities. It is their interests, sense of national needs, political judgments, and hard work that focus a committee's limited time on a legislative agenda.[89]

In the time before a new Congress convenes and in the time immediately afterwards, a committee chair, his or her closest allies, and the chair's party have the most flexibility in determining the key legislative issues that the committee will address in the two-year time frame of a Congress. To wait to identify key legislative issues until later in the first session allows greater opportunity for other individuals and events to determine a committee's agenda. To go forward without knowledge of key legislative issues risks having exigencies and events determine the agenda and having committee resources misallocated by looming deadlines or to lower-priority matters.

## Oversight and Investigations

One of the ways in which congressional committees gather information for possible future lawmaking, inform committee members communally on a topic, and influence the implementation of laws already enacted by Congress is through the conduct of oversight— "continuous watchfulness" in the words of the Legislative Reorganization Act of 1946[90]—and especially the convening of oversight hearings. The rules of the House assign committees responsibility for determining, based on oversight, whether laws within their respective jurisdictions should be changed or if additional laws are necessary.[91]

---

(...continued)

"Entitlement Program—A federal program under which individuals, businesses, or units of government that meet the requirements or qualifications established by law are entitled to receive certain payments if they seek such payments. Major examples include Social Security, Medicare, Medicaid, unemployment insurance, and military and federal civilian pensions. Some entitlements are funded by permanent appropriations, others by annual appropriations.... Congress cannot control the expenditures for entitlement programs by refusing to appropriate the sums necessary to fund them, because the government is legally obligated to pay eligible recipients the amounts to which the law entitles them.... Under many entitlement programs, spending automatically increases or decreases over time as the number of recipients eligible for benefits varies. Some entitlement benefits are indexed for inflation.... "

From *Congressional Quarterly's American Congressional Dictionary* (Washington, DC: CQ Press, 2001), pp. 219 and 90-91; available online to Congress, at http://www.crs.gov/pages/glossary_a.aspx.

[89] See CRS Report RS20991, *Legislative Planning: Considerations for Congressional Staff*, by Judy Schneider.

[90] 60 Stat. 812, 832.

[91] House Rule X, cl. 2. For a substantive overview of procedures and resources for committees' conduct of oversight, see CRS Report RL30240, *Congressional Oversight Manual*, by Todd Garvey et al. In this report, the authors list some of the purposes of oversight of the executive: ensure executive compliance with legislative intent; improve the (continued...)

---

Among the requirements for committees' reports' contents under House rules, reports on measures are to include oversight findings and recommendations.[92]

House rules require *each committee* to hold an open meeting, with a quorum present, *to adopt an oversight plan for a two-year Congress by February 15 of the first session of a Congress*, and to submit the plan to the Oversight and Government Reform Committee and the House Administration Committee.[93] Committees are also directed in House rules to establish oversight subcommittees or to assign to subcommittees responsibility for oversight.[94]

Preparation of an oversight plan requires immediate attention to accurately reflect a committee's oversight priorities. The plan, however, is not a straitjacket in limiting oversight to subjects listed in the plan or requiring oversight action on every subject listed. Committees have tended to include a broader set of oversight subjects in their plans than it is likely they can cover in a two-year Congress. However, preparation of the plan is a key opportunity for the chair, subcommittee chairs, and other committee members to determine what oversight they consider critically important, particularly as it relates to the committee's legislative priorities.

With an identification of critical oversight subjects, a committee can make assignments to and establish schedules for committee staff, agency and program staff, GAO, and other entities that support the committee in its oversight function.[95]

---

(...continued)

efficiency, effectiveness, and economy of government operations; evaluate program performance; prevent executive encroachment on legislative prerogatives and powers; investigate alleged instances of poor administration, arbitrary and capricious behavior, abuse, waste, dishonesty, and fraud; assess agency or officials' ability to manage and carry out program objectives; review and determine federal financial priorities; ensure that executive policies reflect the public interest; protect individual rights and liberties; and other specific purposes, such as monitoring the use of contractors and consultants for government services, and investigating constituent complaints.

In addition to general oversight responsibilities, "special oversight functions" are assigned to the Appropriations, Armed Services, Budget, Education and the Workforce, Energy and Commerce, Foreign Affairs, Homeland Security, Natural Resources, Oversight and Government Reform, Rules, Science, Space, and Technology, Small Business, and Permanent Select Intelligence Committees. Rule X, cl. 3. Additional oversight authority is found at Rule XI, cl. 1(b).

The Appropriations, Budget, Oversight and Government Reform, and House Administration Committees are assigned "additional functions" by House rules. Rule X, cl. 4(a), (b), (c), and (d), respectively. Each standing committee is assigned responsibilities, in conjunction with its consideration of legislation, for reviewing appropriations made for federal programs and activities. Rule X, cl. 4(e). Each standing committee is also assigned responsibility for reviewing tax policies affecting subjects within their jurisdiction. Rule X, cl. 2(c).

The Permanent Select Committee on Intelligence is assigned certain duties under Rule X, cl. 11. The duties of the Ethics Committee are detailed in Rule XI, cl. 3.

The Speaker may also appoint ad hoc oversight committees with House approval. Rule X, cl. 2(e).

[92] House Rule XIII, cl. 3(c)(1).

[93] House Rule X, cl. 2(d)(1). Rule X, cl. 2(d)(2) directs the Oversight and Government Reform Committee to consult chamber leaders and report the committees' oversight plans and the Oversight and Government Reform Committee's recommendations to the House.

[94] House Rule X, cl. 2(b)(2).

[95] In addition to publishing the Congressional Oversight Manual, the Congressional Research Service organized a three-day program, *Congressional Oversight: A "How-To" Series of Workshops*, on June 28, July 12, and July 26, 1999. Videotapes of all the workshop sessions are available from an author of the *Oversight Manual,* Walter Oleszek, CRS Senior Specialist in American National Government. Proceedings were published as a committee print: U.S. Congress, House Committee on Rules, *Congressional Oversight: A "How-To" Series of Workshops*, committee print, 106th Cong., 1st sess., (Washington, DC: GPO, 2000).

---

In addition, Congress has created entities, such as GAO, the inspectors general, and CRS, that are specifically directed to inform Congress through written reports and oral communications. Congress has also placed reporting requirements in numerous statutes, providing Congress with an enormous flow of information from the executive branch. These and other resources' intellectual capital—analysts, attorneys, economists, other specialists, written reports, and consultative services—provide a committee with a "running start" in establishing oversight priorities and informing the committee about issues affecting agencies and programs within the committee's jurisdiction.[96]

Congressional oversight can be viewed as a continuum of activities that in its most potent expression is the investigative power of Congress. Congressional investigations might include the use of subpoenas;[97] discussions with witnesses' attorneys; witnesses invoking constitutional privileges in order not to testify;[98] the invoking of executive privilege;[99] and the threat of citation, or citation, by the House of a witness for contempt. Early and careful planning, consistent application of committee resources, highly capable committee staff, and perseverance are some attributes associated with successful congressional committee investigations.[100]

## Approving/Disapproving Executive Proposals

Congress has passed a number of laws that provide mechanisms for approving or disapproving executive proposals. These laws sometimes address specific legislation and sometimes address a class of proposal. For example, the President had trade negotiating authority under the Trade Act of 2002 until June 30, 2007 (P.L. 107-210). Using this authority, the President negotiated certain trade agreements to be considered in Congress under expedited congressional procedures established in trade laws. Other laws, such as the Congressional Review Act (P.L. 104-121, subtitle E), contain a procedural mechanism for Congress to review and disapprove proposed federal agency rules.[101]

---

[96] See also CRS Report RL33151, *Committee Controls of Agency Decisions*, by Louis Fisher; and CRS Report RS22132, *Legislative Vetoes After Chadha*, by Louis Fisher.

[97] Authority for committees to issue subpoenas and swear in witnesses is contained in House Rule XI, cl. 2(m). On two related procedural matters, privilege accorded to resolutions of inquiry is contained in Rule XIII, cl. 7, and the process for questions of privilege is contained in Rule IX.

[98] See CRS Report RL34114, *Congress's Contempt Power and the Enforcement of Congressional Subpoenas: A Sketch*, by Todd Garvey and Alissa M. Dolan; and CRS Report RL34097, *Congress's Contempt Power and the Enforcement of Congressional Subpoenas: Law, History, Practice, and Procedure*, by Todd Garvey and Alissa M. Dolan.

[99] See CRS Report R42670, *Presidential Claims of Executive Privilege: History, Law, Practice, and Recent Developments*, by Todd Garvey and Alissa M. Dolan.

[100] The Congressional Research Service organized a day-long conference on oversight and investigations on October 28, 2004. Videotapes of all the workshop sessions are available from Walter Oleszek, CRS Senior Specialist in American National Government: (1) Oversight: A Key Constitutional Function; (2) Planning Investigative Hearings: Strategic Considerations; (3) The Rules and Tools of Oversight; (4) The Role of GAO and the Inspector General in Oversight; and (5) Congress Oversees the Intelligence Community.

[101] For the text of public laws containing legislative procedures enacted in law, see *House Manual*, pp. 1107-1273. See also CRS Report RL30599, *Expedited Procedures in the House: Variations Enacted Into Law*, by Christopher M. Davis; and CRS Report RL31160, *Disapproval of Regulations by Congress: Procedure Under the Congressional Review Act*, by Richard S. Beth.

---

As a committee contemplates its agenda, it seeks to be aware of pending and potential executive proposals that might be within the committee's jurisdiction and subject to congressional approval or disapproval.

## Author Contact Information

Judy Schneider
Specialist on the Congress
jschneider@crs.loc.gov, 7-8664

Michael L. Koempel
Senior Specialist in American National Government
mkoempel@crs.loc.gov, 7-0165